THE WORLD
IN THE TIME OF
ALBERT EINSTEIN

Chelsea House Publishers
Philadelphia

FIONA MACDONALD

First published in hardback edition in 2001
by Chelsea House Publishers, a subsidiary of
Haights Cross Communications. All rights reserved.
Printed and bound in China.

First published in the UK in 1997 by
Belitha Press Limited, London House,
Great Eastern Wharf, Parkgate Road,
London SW11 4NQ, England

Text copyright © Belitha Press 1997
Text by Fiona Macdonald
Map by Robin Carter, Wildlife Art Agency

Editor: Christin Hatt
Series Editor: Claire Edwards
Design: Jamie Asher
Art Director: Helen James
Picture Researcher: Diana Morris
Consultant: Sallie Purkiss

First printing
1 3 5 7 9 8 6 4 2

The Chelsea House World Wide Web
address is: http://www.chelseahouse.com

Library of Congress Cataloging-in-Publication Data applied for.

ISBN: 0-7910-6031-4

Picture acknowledgements:
AKG London: 5b Erich Lessing, 6t, 6b, 7, 22b & 23 Dorothea Lange.
Bridgeman Art Library: 21t Private Collection, 33b Armoury Museum,
Kremlin, Moscow.   Camera Press: 25   A.Bailey.   Corbis Bettmann: 15.
E.T. Archive: back cover, 12, 28b Bakelite Museum, 29b, 37t Reina Sofia
Museum Madrid © Sucession Picasso Paris & DACS London 1998, 45b
Museum African & Oceanic Art, Paris.   Getty Images Ltd: front cover r, 5t,
16t, 17, 18, 24t, 26, 37b, 39t, 40, 44, 45t.   David King Collection: 43t.
Peter Newark's Pictures: 1, 2, 3, 4, 13t, 13b, 14t, 14b, 19t, 21b, 24b, 27tl, 27tc,
28c, 29t, 30t, 31, 32, 38t, 38b.   Norsk Sjøfartsmuseum Oslo: 33t.   North
Wind Picture Archives: 19b, 27b.   Popperfoto: 22t, 42.   Retrograph Archive
Ltd, London: front cover l, 20, 30b, 34, 43b.   Spectrum Colour Library: 41b.
Trip: 41t D. Saunders.   Zefa: 16b, 28tr Heilman/Runk/Schoenberger.

CONTENTS

ABOUT THIS BOOK

This book tells the story of Albert Einstein and looks at what was happening all around the world in his time. To help you find your way through the book, each chapter has been divided into seven sections. Each section describes a different part of the world and is headed by a color bar. As you look through a chapter, the color bars tell you which areas you can read about in the text below. There is a history time line, to give you an outline of world events in Albert Einstein's time. There is also a science time line, which gives details of the major discoveries and inventions made during the same period. A world map shows some of the most important places mentioned in the book.

On pages 46–47, there is a glossary that explains some of the unfamiliar words used in this book.

THE STORY OF ALBERT EINSTEIN

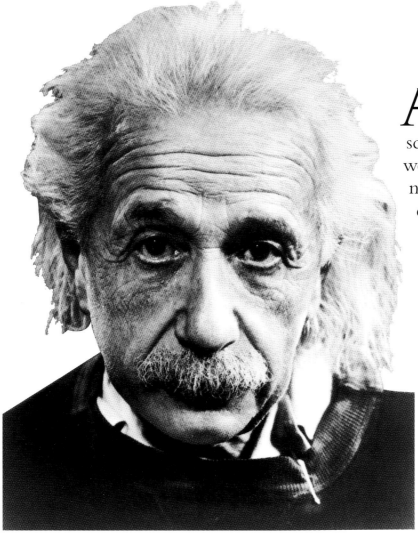

▲ In this photograph, taken around 1950, Albert Einstein looks out with an inquiring gaze. Einstein won worldwide respect and admiration for his achievements as a scientist and his work for peace.

Albert Einstein was one of the most famous scientists who ever lived. He worked out a revolutionary new theory that completely changed the way scientists understand the world. It led to exciting discoveries in space and helped other scientists to develop both deadly weapons and life-saving medical machines. Toward the end of his life, Einstein also became active in politics. This book tells you about his life as a scientist and about his campaigns for justice and peace.

Albert Einstein lived from 1879 to 1955, a time of rapid change. There is no room in this book to describe everything that happened during Einstein's lifetime, but it will tell you about some of the most important events that shaped his world. Many of them still affect the way people live today.

◄ Albert Einstein, aged about 5, and his sister Maja, dressed in the stiff, formal clothes that young children wore for "best" in the late 1800s.

HONEST JOHN

Albert Einstein was born on March 14, 1879, in the city of Ulm, in southern Germany. His father, Hermann, was an engineer, who ran his own business. He brought Albert mathematical puzzles and scientific toys to play with at home—Albert preferred them to story books. Albert's mother, Pauline, was a housewife and a talented pianist. She taught Albert and his sister Maja to love music and encouraged them to work hard at school. Albert did not enjoy school. He did not like its strict rules or organized games. But he did do extremely well in his mathematics lessons. His classmates gave him the nickname "Honest John," because he was very hard-working.

COLLEGE LIFE

In 1896, when he was 17, Albert won a place to study science at a famous college in Switzerland. At the same time he gave up his German citizenship. This was to avoid joining the army, which was compulsory for all German boys. Albert thought war was wicked. He was horrified at the thought that if he became a soldier, he might be ordered to shoot and kill people. For most of his life, he was a pacifist, refusing to fight because he thought it was completely wrong.

A SCIENTIFIC CAREER

In 1900 Albert graduated from college and began to look for a job. For a while he worked as a teacher, which he enjoyed. He also liked going to concerts, playing his violin, and chatting, joking, and discussing the latest scientific ideas with friends. He fell in love with a young woman scientist called Mileva Maric. Later they married and had two sons.

In 1902, Einstein was given a new job as an expert investigator, working for the Swiss government. His task was to check the claims made by inventors who wanted to register new designs. His scientific career had begun.

▼ The equipment-filled laboratory in the Polytechnic School, Zurich, Switzerland, where Albert Einstein taught from 1912 to 1914.

BUSY SCHEDULE

From 1905 to 1915, Einstein was very busy. He continued to study and gave up his government job to become a university professor. He wrote many scientific papers and traveled to many countries. There he taught, met other scientists, and campaigned for justice and world peace.

REVOLUTIONARY RELATIVITY

All this became possible because, in 1905, Einstein had worked out a revolutionary theory. It was called relativity and provided a new way of measuring space, time, and gravity, and of explaining how they work. It solved problems that had puzzled scientists for 200 years and helped them to study the tiny atoms that make up matter. Using this new knowledge, they invented all kinds of devices, from weapons to machines for curing cancer. Einstein's theory also helped astronomers to discover amazing objects in space, such as quasars and black holes.

▲ Einstein teaching university students in the United States toward the end of his life. He was famous for his brilliant, eccentric lectures.

POPULAR PROFESSOR

At first only one professor understood Einstein's theory. But after Einstein published more papers on relativity in 1915, other scientists began to realize that it was true. Einstein became famous. In 1914 he had returned to Germany to take up a post as Director of the Kaiser Wilhelm Institute, the top scientific job in the country. Throughout the 1920s he was awarded prizes in many lands. He was also the world's favorite scientist— ordinary people liked him because he never became too proud and had a sense of humor.

◄ This photograph of Einstein sticking his tongue out at newspaper reporters was taken in the United States in 1951.

▲ Einstein (center) taking part in an antiwar demonstration in Berlin, Germany, in 1923. The demonstration was organized by top scientists from many nations. Like Einstein himself, the world wanted peace.

RISE OF NAZISM

But Einstein's fame could not protect him from a new and terrible danger. In 1932 the Nazi party became powerful in Germany (see page 14). The party aimed to create a "pure" German nation, by exterminating all the people that it thought were not pure, such as gypsies and Jews. Einstein was Jewish and a supporter of the Zionist movement, which campaigned for a Jewish homeland in Israel. He also bravely defended German Jews who protested against Nazi rule. After many threats and attacks, Einstein and his family were forced to flee from Germany. They left for the United States in 1933 and never returned to Europe.

LIFE IN THE UNITED STATES

Americans were proud to welcome someone as clever as Einstein. He was able to continue his teaching and research, and became a professor at Princeton University. He also joined in the fight against the Nazis by helping Americans to develop the world's first atomic bomb. This meant that Einstein had to abandon his pacifist views. But he believed that the Nazis were so evil they had to be defeated at all costs.

A CHANGE OF HEART

Later, when Einstein saw the terrible devastation caused by atomic bombs (see page 14), he called for them to be banned. He also warned people against the dangers of uncontrolled science. He realized that dangerous experiments, scientific accidents, or chemical pollution might one day destroy the whole world. By 1950, Einstein was seriously ill. But he continued with his scientific work, as well as his campaign for world peace. Einstein died in 1955, at the age of 76.

THE WORLD 1879–1955

ABOUT THE MAPS

The maps on this page will help you find your way around the world in Albert Einstein's time. The big map shows some of the places mentioned in the text, including the following:

• **COUNTRIES**, as well as some important states and regions.

• *Peoples*, such as the Mande.

• *GEOGRAPHICAL FEATURES*, including mountains and rivers.

• *Towns and cities* To find the position of a town or city, look for the name in the list below and then find the number on the map.

1	Pearl Harbor	8	Ulm	15	Amritsar
2	Hollywood	9	Berlin	16	Beijing
3	Chicago	10	Sarajevo	17	Shanghai
4	Lakehurst	11	St. Petersburg	18	Vladivostok
5	New York	12	Moscow	19	Hiroshima
6	Guernica	13	Istanbul	20	Melbourne
7	London	14	Johannesburg	21	Sydney

The little map shows the world divided into seven regions. The people who live in a region are linked by customs, traditions, beliefs, or simply by their environment. There are many differences within each region, but the people living there have more in common with one another than with people who live elsewhere. Each region is shown in a different color—the same colors are used in the headings throughout the book.

ARCTIC
OCEAN

BERING SEA

BALTIC
SEA

11

ASIA

12

TRANS-SIBERIAN RAILROAD

SEA OF
JAPAN

9

AUSTRO-
HUNGARIAN
EMPIRE

7

8

OTTOMAN
EMPIRE

BLACK
SEA

CASPIAN
SEA

18

EUROPE

10

13

EMPIRE

16

6

MEDITERRANEAN
SEA

PALESTINE

17

19

SUEZ
CANAL

HIMALAYA
MOUNTAINS

NILE R.

15

PACIFIC

SAHARA

HONG
KONG

OCEAN

AFRICA

INDO-
CHINA

SOUTH
CHINA
SEA

GUAM

Mande

NIGER R.

EQUATOR

JAVA

Aborigines

AUSTRALASIA

14

21

Zulus

CAPE OF
GOOD HOPE

20

Maoris

KEY TO MAP

Africa

Americas

Australasia

East Asia

Europe

Middle East

South Asia

TIME LINE

| 1875 | 1890 | 1900 | 1910 | 1920 |

EUROPE

1875-1898 First Labor Parties founded in many European lands.

1898 Germany plans to become world power. Builds new fleet and enlarges army.

1905 Rebellion in Russia. Czar remains but agrees to some of rebels' demands.

1912-1913 Wars in Balkan lands.

1914-1918 World War I.

1917 Successful Communist revolution in Russia. New nation (USSR) formed in 1922.

1920 League of Nations set up in Geneva, Switzerland, to work for world peace.

AMERICAS

1885 Canadian Pacific Railroad linking east and west coasts completed.

1898 War between U.S. and Spain. U.S. takes over many former Spanish colonies, including Guam, Puerto Rico, and the Philippines (for $20,000,000).

1910-1917 Mexican Revolution.

1912 Transatlantic liner *Titanic* sinks on first voyage.

1914 Panama Canal opens, linking the Atlantic and Pacific Oceans.

1917 U.S. joins in World War I against Germany.

MIDDLE EAST

1906 Rebellion in Persia (modern Iran) against rule of Ottoman Empire.

1908 Oil discovered in Persia.

1908 Young Turk revolution weakens Ottoman Empire.

1916-1918 Arab rebellions against Ottoman Empire.

1917 Balfour Declaration by British government promises Jewish people a homeland in Israel.

AFRICA

1875 Britain buys Suez Canal, Egypt.

1880-1881 First Boer War between Dutch farmers (Boers) and British settlers in South Africa.

1880s-1890s Britain, France, Belgium, and Germany take part in "scramble for Africa."

1886 Gold discovered in South Africa.

1900 Copper mining starts in Katanga (part of the present-day Democratic Republic of Congo).

1899-1902 Second Boer War in South Africa.

1910 Union of South Africa formed.

1912 African National Congress set up by African leaders in South Africa.

1914 Britain takes control of Egypt.

1914-1915 Britain and France conquer German colonies in Africa.

1919 Successful rebellion in Egypt against British rule.

SOUTH ASIA

1876 Queen Victoria of Britain proclaimed Empress of India.

1879 Britain takes control of Afghanistan.

1885 Indian National Congress Party set up to campaign for independence from British rule.

1886 Britain takes control of Burma (Myanmar).

1906 Muslim League set up in India to campaign for independence from British rule.

1919 Peaceful prote killed by British tro Amritsar, India. Der for independence in

EAST ASIA

1894-1895 War between Japan and China. Japan wins some Chinese lands.

1898 Failed attempts at reform in China.

1900 Boxer Rebellion in China.

1904-1905 War between Japan and Russia. Japan wins.

1910 Japan takes control of Korea.

1911 Chinese Revolution. Until 1926, China is ruled by rival warlords.

AUSTRALASIA

1900 Hawaii becomes a territory of the U.S.

1901 All separate states in Australia unite to become a single nation.

1907 New Zealand becomes a dominion—a self-governing country within the British Commonwealth.

1915 Australia and New Zealand send troops to help Britain fight in World War I.

1930   **1940**   **1950**   **1955**

1921 Irish Free State breaks away from British rule.

1933 Hitler becomes Chancellor (head of government) in Germany.

1948 Communists (based in USSR) take over many Eastern European states.

1955 Military alliance of USSR and European Communist states known as Warsaw Pact set up.

1922 Benito Mussolini becomes leader of Italy.

1928 Stalin's first Five Year Plan to reform Russian farms.

1926 General Strike in Britain.

1936-1939 Spanish Civil War.

1942 Holocaust begins in Hitler's Germany.

1939-1945 World War II.

1949 Military alliance of U.S., Canada, and non-Communist European states known as North Atlantic Treaty Organization (NATO) set up. West Germany joins 1955.

1920-1933 Prohibition era in U.S. Leads to increase in organized crime.

1933 U.S. President Roosevelt begins New Deal programs.

1945 United Nations organization founded, with headquarters in New York.

1947 Start of cold war between U.S. and USSR.

1929 Stock Market Crash begins Great Depression in U.S. This spreads to many parts of the world.

1941 U.S. joins in World War II against Germany and Japan following Japanese air attack on Pearl Harbor, Hawaii.

1948 Marshall Plan gives economic aid to friendly European nations damaged by World War II.

1950 McCarthyism—campaign led by Senator Joseph McCarthy against Communists in U.S.—begins.

1923-1924 End of Ottoman Empire. Atatürk sets up nonreligious state in Turkey.
1925 Reza Khan becomes shah (king) of Persia and introduces Western-style reforms.

1932 Kingdom of Saudi Arabia founded.

1936 Oil discovered in Saudi Arabia.
1936 Arabs living in Palestine protest against arrival of Jewish immigrants.

1948 State of Israel set up. First Arab-Israeli War.

1926 Abd el-Krim leads unsuccessful revolt against French and Spanish rule in Morocco.

1939 South Africa joins in World War II to fight against Germany.

1948 Apartheid introduced in South Africa.

1941-1943 Britain and Allies defeat Germans in North Africa.
1945 Unsuccessful revolt against French colonial rule in Algeria.

1952-1959 Mau-Mau rebellion in Kenya against British colonial rule.
1954-1962 War in Algeria against French colonial rule.

1928 Gandhi becomes leader of Indian National Congress Party.

1940 Indian Muslims demand separate state (Pakistan).

1947 India and Pakistan become independent from Britain.

1930 Gandhi leads protests against British salt tax.

1948 Gandhi assassinated.

1948 Burma and Ceylon (modern Myanmar and Sri Lanka) become independent from Britain.

1949 Indonesia becomes independent from Dutch rule.

1921 Chinese Communist Party formed.

1931 Japan conquers Manchuria.

1945 U.S. drops atomic bombs on two Japanese cities. Japan surrenders and World War II ends.

1950-1953 Korean War between Communists and Nationalists.

1927 Chinese Nationalist leader Jiang Jieshi (Chiang Kai-shek) begins fight against Communists.

1934 Mao Zedong leads Chinese Communists on Long March.
1937 War begins between China and Japan.

1946-1949 Civil war in China between Nationalists and Communists. Communists win and set up new state.

1954 Laos, Cambodia, and Vietnam gain independence from France.

1939 Australia and New Zealand join in World War II to fight against Germany.

1951 Australia, New Zealand, and U.S. sign a military alliance known as the ANZUS Pact.

1941 Japan attacks U.S. fleet at Pearl Harbor, Hawaii.

1942 Battle of Midway (north of Hawaii). U.S. navy stops Japan from conquering more Pacific lands.

AROUND THE WORLD

In 1879, when Einstein was born, Europe was the most powerful region on earth, while the United States was rapidly growing richer and stronger. The Ottoman Empire ruled the Middle East, and ancient dynasties governed both Russia and China. But by the end of Einstein's life, in 1955, many European countries had been devastated by two world wars and had lost their overseas colonies. The Middle East was divided among warring states, and Communist revolutions had transformed Russia and China. There were two super-powers, the United States and the USSR.

▲ During World War I, soldiers fought in appalling conditions. This photograph, taken in France in 1916, shows a typical trench—a tunnel dug in the mud where men ate, slept, and sheltered from enemy gunfire.

ENEMIES AND ALLIES

EUROPE

European nations were jealous rivals. They envied one another's armies and navies, colonies, international trade, and industrial wealth. Some countries, such as France and Germany, had a long history of mistrust and war. To support one another, certain groups of nations joined together in alliances. They agreed to defend their allies if any of them was attacked.

▲ A dramatic painting showing
Communist leader Lenin (top right)
leading a protest march at the start
of the Russian Revolution in 1917

WORLD WAR I

In 1914 this system of alliances finally led to war.
In that year Archduke Francis Ferdinand, heir to
the throne of the Austro-Hungarian Empire, was
shot dead in Sarajevo, Bosnia. His assassin was a
Serbian, who wanted independence for Serbs in
Austrian lands. So Austria declared war on Serbia,
and Serbia's ally Russia declared war on Austria.
Austria's ally Germany declared war on Russia
in return. Soon most European countries were
at war. Later Australia, New Zealand, Canada,
and the U.S. joined Britain and France on the
Russian side. The conflict became known as
World War I and lasted until 1918, when Austria,
Germany, and their allies surrendered. In 1919
governments set up the League of Nations, a
society that worked to preserve world peace.

CIVIL WARS

In 1916 Ireland was under British rule. The
Roman Catholic majority in the south wanted
independence, but the Protestant majority in
the north did not. Catholics rebelled against
Britain in the Easter Rising of 1916, and in 1921
Ireland was divided. Six counties in the north
remained British, while the south became self-
governing. Civil war then broke out between
rival groups in the south. In 1937 southern
Ireland became the independent nation of Eire.

Civil war broke out in Spain in 1936 when
General Francisco Franco overturned the elected
government. He wanted to give power to the
king and the army. After three years' fighting,
Franco won. He remained in power until 1975.

THE RUSSIAN REVOLUTION

Most Russians hated their cruel and inefficient
government, which was headed by a royal ruler
called a czar. They were also angry because
ordinary Russians were not allowed to elect its
members. Russians suffered terribly in World
War I. By 1917 many were sick and starving.

In March 1917, civilians and soldiers rioted in
the capital, Petrograd (later St. Petersburg), and
Czar Nicholas II had to resign. In November
more riots broke out, this time organized by the
Bolshevik Party, a Communist group led by
Vladimir Lenin. The Bolsheviks executed the czar
and set up a government run by elected councils,
called soviets. By 1921 the Communists controlled
all Russian lands. They gave them a new name—
the USSR (Union of Soviet Socialist Republics).

JOSEPH STALIN

Lenin died in 1924 and a new Communist
leader, Joseph Stalin, took his place. He was an
extremely cruel ruler, whose grand schemes often
ended in disaster (see page 21). But he remained
in power until his death in 1953.

▲ Nazi leader Adolf Hitler (center) at a rally of supporters in Germany in 1933. He used mass meetings like this to stir up hatred against Jews.

THE RISE OF HITLER

EUROPE

The European nations that won World War I forced Germany to pay huge amounts of money to the countries that it had invaded and to give up the colonies and countries that it had once ruled. Many German people wanted a leader who would make their nation great again. In 1933, Adolf Hitler was named Chancellor of Germany. He enlarged the army and persecuted the Jews. Then, in 1936, he began to occupy nearby land. His aim was to conquer the world.

WORLD WAR II

Hitler was supported by Benito Mussolini, the dictator who ruled Italy, and by Francisco Franco, the army commander who ruled Spain. The government of Japan supported Hitler, too. But many other nations, including Britain and France, joined together to fight against him, and in 1939 World War II began. In 1941, Hitler tried to conquer Stalin's USSR. He failed, and the Soviets became his enemies. In the same year Japanese airplanes bombed American warships in Pearl Harbor, Hawaii. This made the U.S. join in the war against Hitler, too.

THE POSTWAR WORLD

World War II ended in 1945, after an American airplane dropped the first atomic bomb on Hiroshima, Japan. Hitler killed himself, but many other Nazis were put on trial. Germany was divided up between the countries that had defeated it. One part was ruled by the Communist USSR, the rest by Britain, the U.S., and France. Countries conquered by Germany and Japan were freed, but the USSR took over many Eastern European states. To stop communism from spreading, the U.S. gave money and sent experts to rebuild Europe. To prevent more world wars, the United Nations organization was set up in 1945.

▼ American "Flying Fortresses" bomb Germany in 1944. The use of aircraft during World War II meant that, for the first time, whole cities were flattened and millions of ordinary people were killed.

NEW NATIONS

AMERICAS

For over 300 years rival European nations had fought for control of land in North and South America. But by about 1900 almost all the new nations in the Americas had fixed their borders and become self-governing. Canada and British Guiana, however, remained British colonies, and the Caribbean islands were ruled by Britain, the Netherlands, and France.

FIGHT FOR INDEPENDENCE

Most Native Americans in North America had lost their independence. Their last great—and unsuccessful—battle against European settlers took place in 1890 at Wounded Knee, South Dakota. The South American rain forests were hard for settlers to reach, so native peoples there continued their traditional ways of life. But their rights were not protected by law.

RISE OF THE UNITED STATES

By 1900 the U.S. was the world's richest nation. At first, it concentrated on its own affairs. But soon it began to play a major part in international politics. It entered World War I in 1917 (see page 13) and World War II in 1941 (see page 14).

COLD WAR

After World War II ended in 1945, the United States led the fight against Communism in the USSR and China. In 1949 the U.S., Canada, and leading European nations formed the North Atlantic Treaty Organization (NATO). The aim of this military alliance was to defend the West against the Communist threat. Its establishment accented a long period of high tension that began in 1947 between the West and the Communist nations known as the cold war.

► A history lesson in a school in the United States, about 1900. Pupils were allowed to meet Native Americans like this. But most learned about Native American beliefs and customs as though they belonged to the distant past.

FALL OF THE OTTOMANS

MIDDLE EAST

In the 1870s most of the Middle East was ruled by the Ottoman Empire from its capital city, Istanbul. By 1900 it faced threats from two strong neighboring nations—Austria to the west and Russia to the north. Rebels from within the empire also challenged the Ottoman rulers. They wanted to reform the way imperial lands were run. In 1908 a group of army officers and politicians known as the Young Turks rebelled against Sultan Abdul-Hamid II and removed him from power. Under their leadership, the Ottoman Empire fought on the German side in World War I. The empire collapsed when Germany was defeated in 1918.

BIRTH OF ISRAEL

Once Ottoman power ended, Britain and France were given mandates to maintain law and order in several Middle Eastern lands. Zionists (see page 44) claimed the right to a Jewish state in Palestine, a region under British control. This was difficult to achieve as many Christians and Muslims already lived there. A Jewish state, Israel, was created in part of Palestine in 1948, but Jews and non-Jews still quarrel over land there today.

▲ Zulu warriors in the late 1800s. They are wearing traditional feathered headdresses, holding wood and leather shields, and carrying spears called assegais.

SCRAMBLE FOR AFRICA

AFRICA

Until the late 1800s much of Africa was cut off from the rest of the world. But after European explorers brought back news of the continent's size and riches, European nations hurried to seize African lands. In 1884 a conference was held in Berlin, Germany. There European governments took part in the "scramble for Africa," dividing up large areas of African land among themselves. No one consulted African people. Their territories became colonies, and European farmers, miners, and government officials settled on the best land.

◄ The flag of Israel, the nation created after the end of World War II as a homeland for Jewish people who had fled from Nazi persecution

WAR AND REBELLION

There were many African rebellions against European powers. The Zulus fought the British in South Africa in 1879, and a Muslim religious leader, called the Mahdi, fought them in the Sudan in 1885. In 1893 the Mande people of West Africa came into conflict with French settlers along the Niger River.

In South Africa, European settlers clashed with one another. From 1880 to 1881, and from 1899 to 1902, new British settlers and long-established Dutch farmers, known as Boers, fought one another. Britain defeated the Dutch in these Boer Wars, and in 1910 created a new nation, the Union of South Africa. It was independent, but linked to Britain both legally and politically.

▲ Workers at a South African gold mine in 1888. The discovery of diamonds in the country in 1867, and of gold in 1886, fueled European interest in Africa as a whole.

TOWARD INDEPENDENCE

North Africa was a battleground for European armies during World War II. When the war was over, nationalist leaders in many African countries began to demand independence from European rule. In 1945 there was an anti-French rebellion in Algeria. By 1954 it had turned into a war, and many French colonists were killed. Algeria finally achieved independence in 1962. In the British colony of Kenya, Mau Mau warriors attacked British settlers between 1952 and 1955. Kenya eventually became independent in 1963.

COLONIAL RICHES

SOUTH ASIA

European nations ruled many countries in South Asia. France claimed lands in Indochina (modern Cambodia, Laos, and Vietnam), the Netherlands controlled Indonesia, and the British ruled Burma (modern Myanmar) and Malay (now Malaysia). Europeans wanted these lands for their crops, such as spices, coffee, and rubber, and for their metals, such as tin.

JEWEL IN THE CROWN

India was the "jewel in the crown" of the British Empire. But many Indians wanted to govern their own land. In 1885 the mainly Hindu Indian National Congress Party was founded to work for independence. In 1906 the Muslim League was set up to represent Muslims in the campaign.

▼ Indian independence campaigners face British soldiers during a march in Bombay in 1946.

TWO NATIONS

Britain did not want to give India up. In 1919, British troops in Amritsar shot dead hundreds of Indians peacefully campaigning for independence. In 1942 the Congress launched a Quit India Movement, and warned that it might use violence. Faced with the threat of an uprising, Britain granted India independence in 1947. The land was divided into two nations: mainly Hindu India and mainly Muslim Pakistan.

SPREADING NATIONALISM

In the mid-twentieth century, nationalists in other South Asian lands began to demand independence. From 1927 in Indonesia, and from 1946 in Indochina, they rebelled against European rule. They were helped by soldiers hoping to copy Mao Zedong's Communist revolution in China (see page 19). From 1948, Communists also fought the British in Malaya.

BOXER REBELLION

EAST ASIA

During the regency of Qing Dowager Empress Cixi (1862–1908), China faced many problems. Foreign nations, especially Russia, Britain, and France, controlled its trade, and tried to take over its land. Japan attacked its northeastern borders. Some Chinese leaders wanted to reform society by introducing Western science and technology. Others, including Cixi, hated all new ideas.

In 1898 the reformers seized power, but Cixi regained control. In 1900 gangs known as Boxers attacked foreign homes and businesses. Many foreigners were killed, but an army of Americans, Japanese, and Europeans crushed this Boxer Rebellion. In 1912 the last Qing emperor, 6-year-old Puyi, was removed from the throne. A republican government led by Sun Yixian then began to rule the country.

▲ Mao Zedong (left) after the 1934-35 Long March, during which Communists moved from southeastern to northwestern China.

PEOPLE'S REPUBLIC

Sun Yixian soon quarreled with other republican leaders and went into exile. But he returned to head a new government in 1924. From 1927 to 1937, China was torn by civil war between Sun's Republicans; the Revolutionary National Party, led by Jiang Jieshi (Chiang Kai-shek); and the Communist Party, led by Mao Zedong. In 1937 the Japanese invaded the north. Supported by the U.S. and Mao's Communists, Jiang led the fight against Japan. But after Japan was defeated in 1945 (see page 14), the Communist Party won control of China. In 1949 Mao set up the People's Republic, based on Communist principles.

A NEW NATION

Australia and New Zealand changed rapidly during the late 1800s and early 1900s, as many new settlers arrived from Europe. The settlers felt patriotic about their new homelands. The first British governments to rule Australia had divided its vast territory into separate states, run as colonies. But by 1890 the states had won the right to govern themselves. In 1901 they joined together as a new nation, the Commonwealth of Australia.

Britain, Australia, and New Zealand, which the British had granted self-rule in 1856, were linked by recreation, language, and trade. Australian and New Zealand troops also fought to support Britain in both World Wars I and II.

ISLAND COMMUNITIES

Elsewhere in the Pacific, Britain, France, Australia, and New Zealand began to rule islands that had once been independent. They hoped to make money from fishing or mining, or to use the islands' harbors for their long-distance ships.

In 1898 the U.S. acquired Guam from Spain and in 1900 Hawaii. Later these islands played a major part in the fight against Japan during World War II (see page 14). In 1959 Hawaii became a state of the U.S., and Guam is now a self-governing U.S. territory.

► In both Australia and New Zealand, nineteenth-century European settlers built new towns like Adelaide (right) in European style, just like those "back home."

HOW PEOPLE LIVED

◄ Throughout the British Empire everyone owed loyalty to the British monarch. If they could afford it, inhabitants of the empire were expected to purchase "empire produce," such as British factory-made goods, Australian wool, and Indian tea. This food container was made to honor the British queen, Victoria. Behind her two portraits is a map of the vast British Empire.

During Einstein's lifetime many people's lives changed dramatically. The greatest changes happened in Europe and the United States, and in the overseas colonies that European nations ruled. There new mass-production techniques, farm machines, and political ideas, as well as economic crises and the social upheavals caused by two world wars, meant that everyday life was never the same again.

European colonial rule over vast African and Asian empires, together with faster transportation, better communications, and increased trade, meant that, worldwide, people's lives were more closely linked than they had ever been before. But not all people living in European empires were equal. Most Europeans were richer and lived in much better conditions than the native peoples in the lands that they ruled.

▲ British women in 1908, demanding the right to vote. Their campaign succeeded only after they had "proved themselves" by doing men's jobs from 1914 to 1918.

WORKING WOMEN

EUROPE

World War I caused many changes in the lives of European women. In the war they did many jobs that before had been done only by men, such as driving buses. Afterward many still worked in these jobs because, at first, there was a shortage of skilled workers. (Almost 10 million persons had died in the war.) Some people complained, but others viewed women with a new respect. Eventually women in most European countries were given the right to vote on equal terms with men.

ALL CHANGE

The war brought other changes, too. Many people no longer trusted the governments that had led them into such a terrible conflict. New political movements, such as communism, attracted many followers. When Europe was affected by unemployment in the 1920s, then by the Great Depression in the 1930s (see page 22), there were riots and strikes. Many families left to make new lives in colonies overseas.

Joblessness and poverty led governments to develop "welfare states" designed to provide pensions and free medical care for all. In Britain this new system was introduced in 1948.

STALIN'S SCHEMES

In the USSR, Stalin planned grand projects to transform the country. He reorganized villages into huge collective farms to mass-produce grain and built vast steelworks and factories. Stalin made these plans from his headquarters in Moscow, without taking local people's advice. If they did not agree, he sent them to prison. Sometimes Stalin's schemes succeeded. But often they failed, causing pollution and starvation. Millions died in famines in 1921 and 1932.

▼ This Russian propaganda poster shows a worker in front of a new factory. His banner portrays Joseph Stalin (left) and Vladimir Lenin.

AMERICAN DREAM

AMERICAS

In the late 1800s and early 1900s, American bankers, factory owners, oil-well bosses, and property dealers were famous for their know-how and tough talking worldwide. American skyscrapers, apartment buildings, factories, cattle ranches, and farms were bigger than buildings and businesses in most other lands. Big cities were full of enthusiastic immigrants, all eager to work hard, make their fortune, and share in the "American Dream."

▼ By 1933, four years after the crash on the New York Stock Exchange, approximately 15 million people in the U.S. had no work. Many remained jobless for years. This was the depressing scene in a San Francisco unemployment office in 1938.

CITY CRIME

Two problems spoiled this picture of success. The first was crime. In the 1920s new kinds of criminals, known as gangsters, terrorized many American cities. Alcohol was banned in the U.S. during the 1920s, but gangsters ran bars where it was sold illegally. They also ran protection rackets, demanding money to "protect" city businesses from crime. Business owners knew that if they did not pay, the gangsters would destroy their premises. Gangsters also took part in violent gangland wars, during which they murdered their rivals.

◄ Chicago policemen armed with machine guns fought to keep their city streets free of gangsters such as Al Capone.

GREAT DEPRESSION

The second problem was an economic crisis, known as the Great Depression. It started in 1929, when the New York Stock Exchange "crashed." Many businesses collapsed, savers lost their money, and millions of people became unemployed. In 1933, President Franklin D. Roosevelt promised all Americans a "New Deal"—a package of economic benefits and laws. Life then improved for many in the U.S., but the Great Depression continued to cause economic problems in many other countries.

▲ Many American families had
to leave their homes in the 1930s
when farmland turned to dust.

FARMING SUCCESS

Until the 1930s farming boomed in many parts
of North and South America. The fast-growing
population of the U.S., and its highly profitable
businesses, meant that food was in demand and
fetched high prices. Farmers in North America
cleared huge fields and bought high-powered
machines, like tractors and combine harvesters,
to help them work the land. They also started to
use chemical fertilizers to help them grow bigger
crops. In South America, farmers raised huge
herds of cattle and tended vast plantations of
crops such as coffee, cotton, and sugar.

FARMING FAILURE

But in the 1930s American farmers became
poor. The Great Depression meant that they
could only get low prices for their produce. They
had no money to pay for food for their animals,
fuel for their machines, repairs for their buildings,
or rent for their land. Then much of North
America was hit by another disaster. Low rainfall
caused the soil to dry up and turn to dust. High
winds blew it away, leaving just bare, stony
ground, where no crops would grow. Many
families were forced to abandon their farms
and move away in search of work.

FATHER OF THE TURKS

MIDDLE EAST

After the Ottoman Empire collapsed (see page 16), a new government came to power in Turkey in 1923. It was led by an army officer known as Kemal Atatürk, a name that means Father of the Turks. He was determined to set up a non-religious state, ruled by politicians rather than religious laws. Atatürk swept away old Muslim rules. He abolished writing based on Arabic script and replaced it with a new style that used European letters. He also introduced a new education system, new government officials, and new laws. Women were given political rights, and forbidden to wear the Muslim veil. Many new industries were introduced, too, in an attempt to make Turkey like the rich Western world.

▲ Oil was discovered in Persia (modern Iran) in 1908, and in Saudi Arabia in 1936. Soon oil pipelines and automobiles changed the desert way of life forever.

OIL WEALTH

Many other nations in the Middle East kept their traditional Muslim customs and laws, but modernized their economy when oil was discovered. The first oil wells were drilled in Iran and Iraq soon after 1900, with the help of European technicians. Railroads were also built, to carry drums of valuable oil to seaports. For many people in Iran and Iraq, life after the discovery of oil remained much the same as it had always been. They continued to tend flocks of sheep and goats or to grow crops in irrigated fields. But for others oil wealth brought the chance of better housing and education and of more contact with the wider world.

◄ Kemal Atatürk was the first president of the Turkish Republic. He is shown here wearing Western-style clothes, an example he urged all Turkish people to follow.

EUROPEAN COLONIES

AFRICA

For most of Einstein's lifetime, Africa was ruled by European nations. African colonies provided Europe with valuable raw materials, useful goods, and wealth. Some colonies were also useful politically. For example, the Suez Canal in Egypt formed a vital sea link with India, Australia, and New Zealand.

EUROPEAN EXPLOITATION

European colonial governments exploited their African colonies, sending profits from farms, ranches, and gold and diamond mines back to Europe. African people did not benefit. Instead they worked hard for Europeans, growing crops or laboring in mines. A few European missionaries set up schools and hospitals for African people, but most Africans had little chance of a good education or health care.

INTRODUCTION OF APARTHEID

Racism created great problems for many Africans, who did not have the same rights as European colonists. Racist attitudes were particularly extreme in South Africa. In 1948 the South African government introduced apartheid. This was a policy designed to separate black and white people, and to reserve all the best jobs, land, houses, and education for whites.

▼This bridge, in Cape Town, South Africa, was built in accordance with the country's apartheid laws. These were designed to keep people of different races apart. The bridge walkway is divided into two sections, one for whites, the other for nonwhites. Anyone who walked down the "wrong" side could be fined or even arrested and imprisoned.

THE RAJ

SOUTH ASIA

The British colony of India was governed by a huge civil service, led and trained by British men. Their families came to India to live with them, creating a rich, foreign ruling class, known as the Raj. Many members of the Raj made friends with their Indian workers, and with the Indian servants who cared for their children and ran their houses. But few regarded Indian people as their equals. The British relied on friendly Indian princes to help them rule. But they believed that ordinary Indians were not capable of running their country alone.

▼ A maharajah (prince) and his British and Indian guests at a tennis party in 1891. The setting is the city of Kapurthala in the north Indian region of the Punjab. There many princes and ordinary people followed the Sikh religion.

INDIA'S ECONOMY

Many Indian people thought that Britain was damaging India's economy. Indians were not allowed to develop Western-style industries, for fear they would compete with British businesses. As a result, many Indian people were poor. Some worked hard producing cheap raw materials such as cotton to be turned into cloth in Britain. Others grew crops such as tea for Europeans to consume. Many moved to cities and took jobs as longshoremen, shopkeepers, cleaners, or clerks.

MALAYA AND INDONESIA

The situation was very similar in many other European colonies in South Asia. In Malaya large numbers of local people worked on European-owned rubber plantations or as shipping clerks and servants. In Indonesia they worked on coffee plantations or in tin mines.

▲ A rich young noblewoman (left)
and a poor peasant boy in China

RICH AND POOR

EAST ASIA

A few Chinese people
were very rich. They worked as top government
officials or as merchants at international ports
such as Shanghai and Hong Kong. But most
people in China were peasants, who worked very
hard on their farms. Often they barely managed
to survive, and usually they were very poor.
Sometimes crops died, or rival armies fought
across their lands. Then there was famine, and
millions of people starved to death.

COLLECTIVE FARMING

After Communist leaders won control of China
in 1948, they took estates away from wealthy
landlords and divided them among the peasants.
They also killed about 2 million landlords for
treating peasants badly in the past.

By 1950 about 500 million people lived in
China. To produce more food to feed them all,
Chinese leaders copied Stalin's plans (see page
21), introducing collective farming. Later
Chinese villages were encouraged to work
together and share all they owned. But this was
not a success, and for a while farm output fell.

▶ Sheepshearers hard at work on
a big Australian farm in 1891. Fine
merino wool from Australian sheep
was among the best in the world.

GROWTH AND CONFLICT

AUSTRALASIA

By 1890, Europeans in New Zealand and
Australia had occupied almost all the land suitable
for farming and mining. New towns also grew
quickly. Melbourne in Australia had a population
of 29,000 in 1851. By 1891 it was 473,000.

This rapid settlement led to disputes with local
peoples. The Maoris of New Zealand fought the
settlers fiercely and won the right to keep some
of their ancient homelands. But many Maoris
died in the fighting, and by 1896 only about
40,000 were still alive. In Australia the situation
was even worse. Whole communities of Aborigines
died of hunger and European diseases.

FARM PRODUCE

During the early 1900s farmers in Australia and
New Zealand were very successful. Refrigerated
ships carried the meat, butter, and cheese they
produced to shops in Europe and many other
lands. Top-quality Australian wool was also sold
worldwide. But during the 1930s the farmers
suffered badly. The Great Depression in the U.S.
(see page 22) meant that people in other lands
could no longer afford to buy their goods.

DISCOVERY AND INVENTION

During Einstein's lifetime, discoveries and inventions were made at an amazing rate. Some, like Einstein's theories, helped scientists to understand how the universe works. They were pure science— scientific study carried out to increase knowledge, rather than for practical purposes. Others, like televisions and jet airplanes, were very practical.

Many of the discoveries and inventions from this period had a greater effect than anyone could have imagined at first. Gradually computers and antibiotic drugs, electricity and atomic research, have totally changed the way people live.

There is not enough room in this book to list all the inventions and discoveries that were made during Einstein's time. But you can read about some of the most important in this chapter and find out about many more from the special science time line on pages 34-35.

▲ Penicillin, the first antibiotic drug, was discovered in 1928.

◄ A 1950 advertisement for the new Hawker "Interceptor" jet fighter

▼ A sturdy 1930s radio made from the early plastic Bakelite

SPEED, CLIMB and RANGE

Extensive flight tests have proved the P1052 to have superior fighter characteristics. It combines high top speed and rate of climb with excellent handling qualities at all speeds and a range comparable with that of contemporary piston types.

HAWKER
P1052 INTERCEP

HAWKER AIRCRAFT LIMITED

RADIO AND TELEVISION

EUROPE

Communications were changed forever in 1901, when Italian inventor Guglielmo Marconi sent the first long-distance radio waves from Cornwall to Newfoundland. By the 1920s many Europeans had radio sets, and the BBC (British Broadcasting Corporation) made its first radio broadcasts in 1922. Scottish engineer John Logie Baird built the first television in 1926, but his design was replaced by a better version using technology invented by Russian Vladimir Zworykin in 1923.

TRANSPORTATION TRENDS

Until the late 1800s nothing could move faster than a sailing ship. But by 1952, passenger jets could travel close to the speed of sound.

Among the most important transportation inventions of this period were Gottlieb Daimler's gasoline-burning internal combustion engine, motorcycle, and early car, all made in Germany by 1885. His bicycle was built in the same year. In 1888 Scotsman John Boyd Dunlop invented rubber tires for bicycles. Later they were fitted to cars as well. Fast steam locomotives were also invented. The British *Mallard* reached almost 126 mph in 1938.

► On May 6, 1937, the giant German airship *Hindenburg* crashed at Lakehurst, New Jersey, after crossing the Atlantic. Thirty-six people died and many more were injured.

IN THE AIR

There were developments in air travel, too. French aviator Louis Blériot made the first flight across the English Channel in 1909, while British pioneers John Alcock and Arthur Brown made the first nonstop flight across the Atlantic in 1919. British aircraft engineer Frank Whittle invented the jet engine in 1930 and built the first jet airplane in 1937. Gas-filled airships were a popular way to travel until the terrible *Hindenburg* disaster of May 1937 (see above).

Russian scientist Konstantin Tsiolkovsky published designs for rockets between 1903 and 1913, though none was ever built. But by 1944, German rockets were so advanced that they were used to attack London in World War II.

► In 1906, British warship *HMS Dreadnought* was launched. It was one of the earliest steam turbine-powered ships.

LOUIS PASTEUR

Frenchman Louis Pasteur made one of the most important European breakthroughs in medical science. In 1880 he published his discovery that invisible germs—known as bacteria and viruses today—cause disease. He also found that these germs could be killed by heating. This heat treatment, called pasteurization, is still used to make milk safe. Pasteur also developed vaccines to protect humans and animals from diseases such as rabies.

X-RAYS AND ANTIBIOTICS

Wilhelm Röntgen, Marie Curie, and her husband, Pierre, all investigated the X-rays given off by radioactive chemicals. Their discoveries made the modern uses of X-rays possible, such as the examination of broken bones and the killing of faulty body cells that cause cancer and other diseases. In 1928, Scottish doctor Alexander Fleming discovered penicillin, a mold that kills bacteria. It became the first of many antibiotic drugs, which have been used to fight infections and save millions of lives worldwide.

▼ A 1946 American advertisement for rayon, one of the first artificial fibers

▲ The research laboratory at Menlo Park, New Jersey, where Thomas Edison invented the electric light bulb in 1879. He called the building his inventions factory.

INSTANT ELECTRICITY

In 1879, American inventor Thomas Edison invented the electric light bulb. (In Britain Joseph Swan invented a similar bulb in exactly the same year.) Three years later, in 1882, Edison designed the first electricity-generating plant. It was built in New York and was soon copied in other U.S. cities and European countries. This allowed houses, streets, shops, offices, and factories to have light and power at the flick of a switch.

MULTIPURPOSE PLASTICS

In 1910, American inventors produced the first synthetic plastics. They could be used to make all kinds of objects, from boats and buildings to scientific instruments and sandwich wrappings. Synthetic fibers, like nylon, also had many uses. The first nylon stockings went on sale in the U.S. about 1940. Nylon was also used for parachutes to save airmen's lives in World War II.

◄ Model T cars being mass-produced at the Ford factory, Detroit, in 1925. Each car was exactly the same. Engineer Henry Ford once said that his customers could buy the cars "in any color they like—so long as it's black."

CAR CULTURE

In 1913 engineer Henry Ford designed the world's first production line for his factory, to make Model T cars. Parts for each car traveled down a conveyor belt. The workers stood alongside, performing their own tasks. By the time the car reached the end of the production line, it was fully assembled and ready to drive. This way of making things was quicker and cheaper than old-fashioned craft techniques.

COMPUTER POWER

The first electronic computer was built in 1939 by American John V. Atanasoff. In 1943 an electronic computer was built secretly in Britain to break codes in wartime. The next, the ENIAC, became famous. Built in the U.S. in 1946, it could do 5,000 calculations per second but filled a room. After American engineers at Bell Labs invented transistors in 1948, computers could be made much smaller.

TRAVEL AND TRANSPORTATION

Improvements in shipping made it easier for Americans to export foods and factory-made goods. The Panama Canal, completed in 1914, allowed cargo ships to sail from the Atlantic to the Pacific Ocean quickly, without making the long journey around the tip of South America.

In 1903 the world's first powered flight was made by American brothers Orville and Wilbur Wright. In 1927, American Charles Lindbergh made the first nonstop solo flight across the Atlantic Ocean. In 1947, Charles Yeager flew an American jet faster than the speed of sound.

FAST FOODS

Several new ways of selling and processing foods were invented by Americans during this time. In 1916 the first self-service supermarket opened in the U.S. After experiments in Alaska in 1925, Clarence Birdseye marketed frozen food. In 1947, American shops began to sell microwave ovens.

► Jewish settlers using mules to plow the field of Armageddon (Megiddo) in Israel in 1934. New farming methods enabled them to grow food crops in the desert.

DESERT FARMS

MIDDLE EAST

In the new state of Israel, the land was dry and rocky. From the 1940s onward, settlers on communal farms called kibbutzim looked for new ways of farming that would "make the desert bloom." They drilled wells, dug irrigation ditches, and experimented with methods of removing salt from sea water to make it suitable for watering crops. Later they also introduced new crops, such as avocados.

FARMS, MINES, AND WELLS

AFRICA

European farmers, hoping to get rich, introduced crops from abroad to African lands. But much greater wealth came from Africa's rich mineral deposits. The British explorer Cecil Rhodes discovered gold and diamonds in southern Africa in the late 1800s. People had known about the copper in Zambia and Congo for centuries. But it was only in the early 1900s, when these countries were under European rule, that the minerals were mined in large quantities. Europeans organized the mining companies, but most of the dirty, dangerous work was done by badly paid Africans.

RAIL TRAVEL

Africa's first railroads were built during Einstein's lifetime, mainly to help European farmers, ranchers, and mine owners move their goods to seaports for export around the world. One of the earliest was the Kenya to Uganda railroad in East Africa, which was completed in 1903. It also carried thousands of European settlers from the coast to their new homes inland. African and Indian laborers constructed this railroad. When it was eventually completed, most of the Indian workers returned to their homeland.

JAVA MAN

SOUTH ASIA

In 1859, British naturalist Charles Darwin suggested that humans and apes might be descended from a common ancestor. Since then scholars have worked hard to discover if this was true. In the late 1800s and early 1900s, they made expeditions to remote places, hoping to find ancient human remains. In 1891 explorers on the island of Java, Indonesia, found bones from a creature they called Java Man. The bones did not come from a modern type of human, but from a human ancestor known as *Homo erectus*.

JAPANESE SHIPBUILDERS

EAST ASIA

During the late 1800s and early 1900s, Japanese politicians and businessmen were eager to learn about Western discoveries and inventions and to introduce them to Japan. In the late 1800s they opened up many new ports to trade with Europe. Ships were the most important means of international travel, so the Japanese became expert shipbuilders, and Japanese companies owned some of the largest cargo-carrying fleets in the world. Japanese engineers also copied and improved Western railroad technology—by 1906 a rail network had been built across their country.

TRANS-SIBERIAN RAILROAD

Even before the 1917 revolution (see page 13), Russia controlled many East Asian lands. The harbor at Vladivostok, on the coast of the Sea of Japan, gave Russian territories in Mongolia and Siberia an outlet for trade with these nations, especially Japan. In 1891, Russian engineers began to build the Trans-Siberian Railroad. It was designed to link Vladivostok with Moscow, the Russian capital, far to the west. When completed in 1916, it was the longest railroad in the world.

▶ This gold model of a Trans-Siberian Railroad train, and its egg container, were made by Peter Carl Fabergé.

▲ Roald Amundsen and his team stand beside the South Pole in 1911. Their huskies rest in the background.

ANTARCTIC EXPEDITIONS

AUSTRALASIA

In 1911 two rival expeditions left New Zealand with the aim of crossing the Antarctic ice cap to reach the South Pole. No one had ever made the journey before. Norwegian explorer Roald Amundsen carried tents and food on sleds pulled by huskies, reached the Pole quickly, and returned in triumph. British explorer Robert Scott used ponies to carry his supplies, and took about five weeks longer to reach the Pole. He died from cold, hunger, and exhaustion on the return journey.

AIR TRAVEL

The invention of aircraft made it easier to travel to Australia, and to cross the vast distances within the country. In 1930 British pilot Amy Johnson flew to Australia on her own. Her flight was halted several times for repairs and took 19 days. But it encouraged other adventurers to travel by air. Within Australia, aircraft and two-way radios that used Morse Code made it possible to set up a flying doctor service in 1928. This brought medical care to the outback. Radios were also used to beam school lessons to children there.

SCIENCE TIME LINE

1879

1885   Louis Pasteur (France) develops vaccine against rabies.
1889   Eiffel Tower, the world's tallest wrought-iron building, constructed in Paris.
      1895   Wilhelm Röntgen (Germany) discovers X-rays.

1900

1900   Max Planck (Germany) formulates quantum theory,
which helps to explain the structure of atoms.
1901   Guglielmo Marconi (Italy) transmits radio waves across the Atlantic Ocean.
1903   Orville Wright (U.S.) makes first flight in a powered aircraft.
1906   Roald Amundsen (Norway) makes journey through the Northwest Passage,
a route from the Atlantic to the Pacific Ocean, around the top of North America.

1914   Panama Canal completed, linking Atlantic and Pacific Oceans.

1920

1921   Albert Einstein (U.S.) wins Nobel Prize for Physics.
1923   Louis Victor de Broglie (France) publishes Wave Particle
Theory, which helps to explain how light and energy behave.

1927   Charles Lindbergh (U.S.) makes first New York–Paris solo flight, in 33.5 hours.
1928   Alexander Fleming (Scotland) discovers penicillin, the world's first antibiotic.
1929   German airship makes first round-the-world flight.

1930

1930   Frank Whittle (Britain) patents gas turbine engine, used in 1937 to power jets.
1931   Auguste Piccard (Switzerland) makes first balloon flight into stratosphere.

1934   Ocean liner *Queen Mary* launched. Soon holds speed record for crossing the Atlantic Ocean in just under 4 days.
1935   Robert Watson-Watt (Scotland) invents radar system for navigation.
1938   Laszlo Bíró (Hungary) invents first usable ballpoint pen.
1939   Igor Sikorsky (U.S.) builds first practical helicopter.

1940

1943   Jacques Cousteau (France) invents aqualung for deep-sea diving.
1944   Germans use high-altitude V-2 rockets to attack London.
1945   U.S. drops world's first atomic bombs on Japan.

1947   Charles Yeager (U.S.) flies faster than the speed of sound.

1949   USSR explodes its first atomic bomb.

1950

1952   British Comet becomes first passenger jet plane.
1953   Charles Townes (U.S.) invents maser, forerunner of laser.

1953   Edmund Hillary (New Zealand) and Tenzing Norgay (Nep
make first climb of Everest, the highest mountain on Earth.
1954   First nuclear-powered submarine (U.S.).

1955

1955   Jonas Salk (U.S.) develops vaccine against polio.

1959   St. Lawrence Seaway (U.S.-Canada) completed,
linking the Great Lakes to the Atlantic Ocean.

1883   First skyscraper built, Chicago.
1886   Gottlieb Daimler (Germany) builds gasoline-powered car.

1895   Lumière brothers (France) show first "motion picture" (film).

1900   Sigmund Freud (Austria) publishes *The Interpretation of Dreams*, a pioneering book on how human minds work.
1903   Konstantin Tsiolkovsky (Russia) publishes his first rocket design.

1903   Marie Curie (Poland) and her husband, Pierre (France) win Nobel Prize for their work investigating radioactivity.

1909   Louis Blériot (France) makes first flight across English Channel.

1909   Robert Peary (U.S.) becomes first man to reach North Pole.

1916   Karl Schwarzschild (German) publishes the black-hole theory about mysterious, invisible areas of space.

Charles Chaplin

1923   Vladimir Zworykin (Russia) invents first television tube.
1926   Robert Goddard (U.S.) builds first liquid-propelled rocket.

1926   John Logie Baird (Scotland) designs first television set.
1927   First "talking picture" (film with sound) (U.S.).

1930   Paul Dirac (Britain) publishes Particle Theory. It helps scientists to understand how atoms are made.

1931   Karl Jansky (U.S.) pioneers radio astronomy (studying space by observing energy waves sent out by stars).

1935   Wallace Carothers (U.S.) invents nylon, the world's first "test-tube" fiber.

1934   Charles Beebe (U.S.) dives 3,028 feet under the sea in a bathysphere, setting a new depth record.

1939   Paul Müller (Switzerland) invents chemical insecticide DDT.

1940   Britain's RAF pilots fly new Spitfire fighter planes to defend UK from German air attack.

1942   American physicists build first nuclear reactor and produce first controlled chain reaction.

1946   ENIAC computer built in U.S.
1947   Dennis Gabor (U.S.) invents holograms.
1948   Bell Labs engineers (U.S.) invent transistor.

1953   James Watson (U.S.) and Francis Crick (Britain) discover double helix structure of DNA, an important substance that carries genetic information in all living cells.

THE CREATIVE WORLD

FELIZ AÑO NUEVO

Before Einstein's lifetime artists, musicians, and architects in many lands had created works of art in distinctive local styles for thousands of years. Sometimes they borrowed ideas and techniques from distant countries, but their own special designs stayed basically the same. But by the end of Einstein's life, there had been a revolution in the arts. New media—movies, radio, phonograph records, and cheap color printing—were carrying songs, dances, fashions, and designs to a mass audience, worldwide. Styles just kept on changing, too, more and more quickly.

▶ This Spanish New Year card from the 1920s shows a fashionable young woman standing beside a phonograph. For the time her clothes are very daring. Her dress is short, sleeveless, low-necked, and loose around the waist. Her short hair is bobbed in the latest style.

◄ Pablo Picasso painted *Guernica* in 1937 to protest the town's bombing in the Spanish Civil War.

▼ Russian ballet dancer Vaslav Nijinsky was famous for his dramatic style.

ART STYLES

EUROPE

All over Europe, painters were experimenting with new styles. Art no longer aimed to show people, places, and objects as they really appeared. Instead artists invented new ways of depicting ideas and feelings in their work. In France, Édouard Manet, Claude Monet, and others painted in a dreamy style that used hazy blocks of color instead of hard, sharp outlines. This was known as Impressionism. Other artists, like Spaniard Pablo Picasso and Frenchman Georges Braque, invented a new style of painting called Cubism. Cubist paintings showed objects from many different viewpoints all at once. Belgian René Magritte and Spaniard Salvador Dali were two of the most important Surrealist artists. They painted a strange, unreal world to shock people and make them think.

NEW DESIGNS

In Germany artists and craft workers belonging to a college called the Bauhaus experimented with streamlined industrial designs. In Britain sculptors like Henry Moore carved stone statues in curving shapes. French architect Le Corbusier designed the first high-rise apartment buildings.

MUSIC AND DANCE

There were also many new ideas in music and dance. Composers such as Arnold Schönberg, Benjamin Britten, and Dmitri Shostakovitch experimented with a new musical scale. Claude Debussy attempted to create "Impressionist" music—patterns of tones and moods. Igor Stravinsky caused a riot when his startling ballet music *The Rite of Spring* was first performed in Paris in 1913. Other new ballets caused outrage with their spiky movements. Nationalistic composers, such as Jean Sibelius of Finland, used legends and folk songs to inspire their work.

LITERARY LIFE

There were new trends in literature, too. Dramatists like Henrik Ibsen, Anton Chekhov, and George Bernard Shaw wrote plays about real-life issues, such as poverty. English writers such as Wilfred Owen, horrified by the suffering of World War I, wrote many poems and novels calling for peace.

POPULAR ENTERTAINMENT

AMERICAS

The United States set the trends in popular entertainment. Hollywood was the world center of filmmaking. Until 1927 most films were silent. But then talking pictures, known as "talkies," began to draw vast crowds to movies.

From the 1920s to the 1940s, radio and phonograph records spread American music styles, such as jazz and blues, to many countries. American dances like the Charleston, American dance tunes played by big bands, and American "crooners"—soloists who sang in a romantic style—were also very popular. By the mid 1950s, American rock-and-roll stars like Chuck Berry and Elvis Presley were famous everywhere.

▼ The Cotton Club, New York, in the 1930s. The world's leading jazz musicians and dancers performed there.

► A souvenir postcard of New York's Chrysler Building, which was completed in 1930. It was decorated in ceramic tiles in the fashionable Art Deco style of the time.

MODERN ARCHITECTURE

American architecture was famous for its exciting new designs. In big cities like New York and Chicago, architects built skyscrapers made of steel, glass, and concrete. They used the latest technology to make these structures taller and taller. The Empire State Building in New York was completed in 1931. At 1,472 feet, it was the tallest skyscraper ever built. American architect Frank Lloyd Wright won praise—and criticism—for designing stark, geometric buildings. They still influence many architects working today.

CRITICAL CARTOONS

MIDDLE EAST

In many Middle Eastern countries, art and politics were closely linked. Political cartoons in newspapers were very popular, and thousands were published between 1900 and the 1930s. They usually supported political reformers and opposed strict, old-fashioned governments, as well as interfering Europeans. Middle Eastern artists—especially in Turkey—also worked on huge propaganda posters and statues. These were designed to create a strong image for dynamic new rulers such as Kemal Atatürk.

▲ Dancers and musicians from the West African nation of Sierra Leone, photographed about 1900. The masked man in the center is a traditional healer.

TRADITIONAL DESIGNS

AFRICA

Throughout Africa, builders continued to create beautiful houses. Weavers, potters, and woodcarvers made fabrics, pottery, clay sculptures, masks, and wooden statues in traditional designs. Some of these objects were used to decorate the homes of the rich; others were for religious use. African artists also used their skills to decorate European-style buildings, such as churches and hospitals. European colonial rulers built European-style cities. Among them was the gold-mining town of Johannesburg, South Africa, which was founded in 1886.

In Islamic countries in North and West Africa, mosques, schools, and universities were built in a mixture of African and Middle Eastern styles.

AFRICA ABROAD

African achievements were admired by creative people in many other lands. In Europe the Spanish painter and sculptor Pablo Picasso studied African carvings and masks and copied them in many of his works. In the American South, where many African Americans lived, traditional African music mingled with European-American music to create the blues and jazz.

ANCIENT AND MODERN

SOUTH ASIA

In India ancient themes were used in a modern way. Popular films, full of exciting battles, singing, and dancing, retold ancient myths and legends. Industrial printing presses produced brightly colored posters, showing gods and goddesses, saints and heroes, which ordinary people could use to decorate their homes. Craft workers still produced the fine cloth that had made India famous for thousands of years. But now the thread that they used was factory-made, and the dyes contained chemicals, instead of plants and other natural materials.

EAST MEETS WEST

Easier, faster travel between continents, as well as international newspapers, magazines, and radio programs, made many Indian dancers, poets, and musicians famous in Europe, the U.S., and beyond. Dancer Uday Shankar performed in Europe with leading ballerinas such as Anna Pavlova, and worked to preserve Indian traditional dances at home. Poet Rabindranath Tagore won the Nobel Prize for Literature in 1913, founded schools and a university, and traveled around the West giving lectures about Indian civilization.

JAVANESE ARTS

Many other traditional South Asian arts became well-known and admired in Western lands. These included dyed fabrics known as batiks, from the Indonesian island of Java, and gamelan orchestras —groups of musicians playing bells and gongs.

▼ Dancers from the Indonesian island of Bali. Using elegant gestures, they tell ancient stories about gods and kings.

CHINESE ARTS AND CRAFTS

In China many expensive and beautiful art and craft objects were produced for Empress Cixi's court. They included jade vases, carved golden thrones, delicate flower paintings, glittering jewelry, silken carpets, and magnificent embroidered robes. In 1888 a new Summer Palace was built north of the capital city, Beijing. The empress and her courtiers went there every year to escape the midsummer heat. The palace included an 80-foot-long, boat-shaped summerhouse in the middle of a lake. This was made of pure white marble.

After the Chinese royal family was overthrown in 1912, many of these beautiful objects were destroyed. For a time, while rival warlords fought to control China, new forms of art took their place. These included vivid propaganda posters and dramatic woodcuts showing battle scenes.

◄ Empress Cixi's Summer Palace, including the extraordinary boat-shaped summerhouse (left), was built using funds that were intended for modernizing the navy. The palace was damaged by European troops during the Boxer Rebellion of 1900, but restored three years later.

EUROPEAN TRADITIONS

AUSTRALASIA

When European settlers arrived in Australia, New Zealand, and some Pacific islands, they brought their own cultural traditions with them. For many years local Australasian music, stories, legends, arts, and crafts were ignored or despised, while farms, schools, churches, and homes were built to European designs. Some of these structures were very impressive, for example, the splendid, 1,650-foot-span Sydney Harbour Bridge, which was completed in 1932.

CHANGING ATTITUDES

Aborigine artists in Australia and Maori craft workers in New Zealand continued to produce work in traditional styles, but it was not appreciated by many people, either at home or abroad. But from around 1950, attitudes began to change. Led by painter Sidney Nolan, Australian artists whose ancestors had come from Europe began to paint pictures that were inspired by Australian history and the magnificent Australian landscape. Meanwhile scholars began to understand the important part traditional paintings, carvings, stories, dances, and songs played in both Aborigine and Maori life.

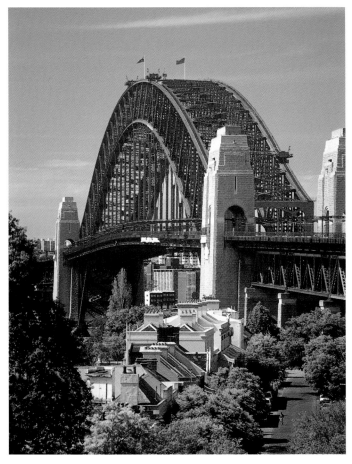

▲ When it opened in 1932, Sydney Harbour Bridge was greatly admired because its design combined technical skill with artistic flair. The tall pillars at each end of the bridge were intended to look like 1930s-style skyscrapers.

BELIEFS AND IDEAS

During Einstein's lifetime traditional beliefs in many parts of the world were challenged and often replaced by new, nonreligious ideas. The more scientific discoveries were made, the more they seemed to explain away the mysteries of the universe and remove people's need to believe in an all-powerful God. But after Einstein's Theory of Relativity was published, many people felt that nothing was certain, not even rational scientific beliefs. They preferred to put their trust in individual human feelings, or in practical political ideas.

▲ When the first atomic bomb was dropped on Hiroshima, Japan, in 1945, people were astonished— and alarmed—by its power. They quickly realized that humans now had the means to destroy the earth.

► The membership badge of the Communist Party. It is decorated with a hammer and a sickle—symbols of workers' power.

RELIGIOUS DECLINE

EUROPE

In Christian Europe the political revolutions and social upheavals of the 1920s and 1930s (see pages 12–14) shook people's beliefs. Many became atheists. Others joined political groups, such as the Communist Party.

Many organizations tried to fill the gap left by religion. People shocked at the suffering caused by wars, floods, and famines set up societies to care for their victims. After World War I, international organizations like the League of Nations were established to work for peace. The Eastern beliefs of Hinduism and Buddhism also became popular in Europe at this time.

LAND OF THE FREE

AMERICAS

In 1886 a huge steel and concrete statue of a woman carrying a flaming torch was set up on an island at the entrance to New York harbor. This was the Statue of Liberty. Liberty means freedom, and American people believed that their country was "the land of the free." People living there—including the millions of immigrants who had arrived in the late 1800s and early 1900s—were free to follow their own religions and make their own laws. They could also express their thoughts openly, because they had the right to free speech. Most Americans were Protestant Christians, but there were also many people of other religions, including Roman Catholics, Mormons, and Jews.

STRONG BELIEFS

Native Americans, who had been turned off their lands, and black families, descended from slaves, did not enjoy this equality. But many drew strength from their religious beliefs. In the late 1800s large numbers of Native Americans joined the Ghost Dance movement, taking part in ceremonies that called on the spirits of dead ancestors to help them reclaim their land.

Many black Americans were Christians. They expressed their hardship, and their trust in God, in moving songs called spirituals. Sometimes traditional African beliefs mingled with their Christian faith. This also happened in South America and the Caribbean. There Christianity, Native American religious ideas, and African beliefs joined to create a new form of worship.

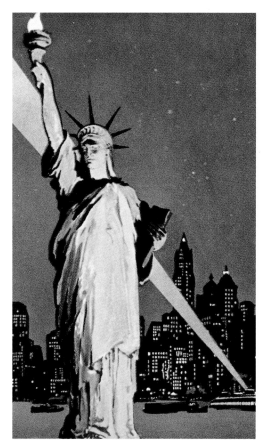

► This American travel poster shows the Statue of Liberty against a dark New York sky, with the lights of the city's skyscrapers shining in the background.

ZIONISM

MIDDLE EAST

Zionists were Jewish people from Europe, the Americas, and Asia, who wanted to create a homeland in Palestine, where Jews had lived thousands of years earlier. Their campaigns led to fighting with other Middle Eastern peoples. These included the Muslim and Christian inhabitants of Palestine and the leaders of nearby kingdoms, who wanted to create a nonreligious, Arabic-speaking state. The Jewish nation of Israel was finally created in 1948.

SAUDI ARABIA

Saudi Arabia was created by people who wanted a homeland where their Muslim faith could be expressed. Between 1902 and 1925, Abd al-Aziz ibn Saud, a member of an old princely family, took control of most of Arabia by settling over 200 religious communities there. Their members farmed the land, organized armies, and made sure Muslim religious laws were kept. They faced opposition from less religious states. But sharia (Muslim holy law) still rules Saudi Arabia today.

RELIGIOUS BELIEFS

AFRICA

There were many types of African religions, but most worshipers shared several major beliefs. They believed in a great creator god and prayed to many lesser gods, too. They also believed in spirits that could help or harm. These could be the souls of dead ancestors, or the "living force" that flowed through the natural world.

From the 1850s onward, Christian missionaries were active in many African countries. As well as teaching their faith, they provided medical care and education. North Africa remained mostly Muslim, as it had been for centuries. But elsewhere various forms of Christianity existed alongside traditional African beliefs.

MAHATMA GANDHI

SOUTH ASIA

Most Indian people were Hindus, but there were also Muslims, Sikhs, Buddhists, Parsees, and Jains. Many put their religious differences aside to campaign for freedom from British rule. The greatest Indian leader, Mohandas Gandhi, was inspired by his Hindu faith to use only non-violent methods in the fight. He encouraged followers to use "truth weapons," such as prayer meetings, hunger strikes, and silent sit-down protests. Gandhi inspired such respect that he was called Mahatma, meaning "Great Soul."

Sadly, after India became independent in 1947, fighting broke out between Hindus and Muslims, and millions of people were killed. Gandhi was murdered by a fellow-Hindu, who thought he was too friendly with people of other faiths.

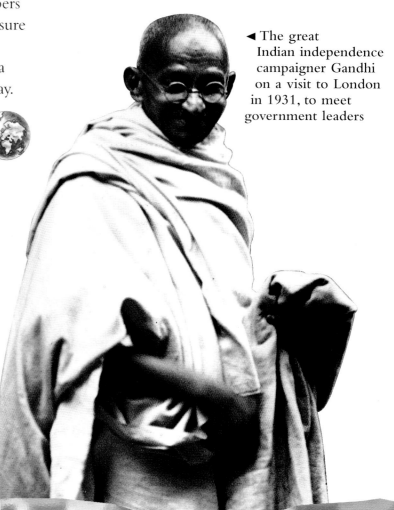

◄ The great Indian independence campaigner Gandhi on a visit to London in 1931, to meet government leaders

▲ Japanese kamikaze pilots were inspired by State Shinto ideas. They bravely flew suicide missions against enemy battleships.

MISSIONARY WORK

European settlers brought their Christian faith to Australia, New Zealand, and the Pacific Islands. They also encouraged Christian missionaries to work among local peoples, in the hope that they would give up their traditional beliefs. The Australian government even introduced a "White Australia" policy. It assumed that the Aborigines and their beliefs and ideas would soon be wiped out by "progress" and a Western way of life.

THE DREAMTIME

In Australia, religious beliefs were centered on the Dreamtime, a long-ago era when the ancestors of all living creatures danced on the earth. In New Zealand, Maori people also honored the spirits of dead ancestors and believed that the gods had blessed certain people and places with magic powers. For many years few white Australians respected these ancient beliefs. But toward the end of Einstein's life, some began to understand their importance and to treat them with respect.

▼ This bark painting was made by Australian Aborigine artist Milingibi.

STATE SHINTO

EAST ASIA

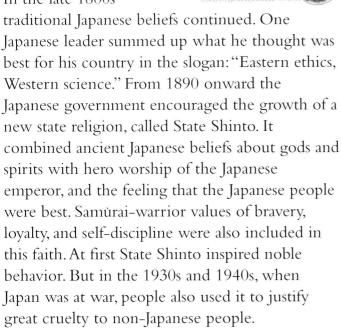

In the late 1800s traditional Japanese beliefs continued. One Japanese leader summed up what he thought was best for his country in the slogan: "Eastern ethics, Western science." From 1890 onward the Japanese government encouraged the growth of a new state religion, called State Shinto. It combined ancient Japanese beliefs about gods and spirits with hero worship of the Japanese emperor, and the feeling that the Japanese people were best. Samurai-warrior values of bravery, loyalty, and self-discipline were also included in this faith. At first State Shinto inspired noble behavior. But in the 1930s and 1940s, when Japan was at war, people also used it to justify great cruelty to non-Japanese people.

GLOSSARY

alliance A friendly agreement between nations or peoples.

ally A friendly person or nation.

antibiotic A drug that kills bacteria (microscopic organisms that can cause disease).

apartheid The South African government policy that was designed to keep people of different races apart. It took away many of black people's rights.

Art Deco A style of art, popular in the 1930s, known for its linear and angular designs.

atheist A person who does not believe in God.

atom one of the tiny particles that make up matter.

atomic bomb A weapon that splits atoms to create an extremely hot, powerful explosion. This gives off deadly invisible rays.

aviator An airplane pilot.

Bakelite An early form of plastic that was hard, brittle, and shiny.

batik A technique used to print cloth. Wax is applied to some areas of the cloth before it is dyed. The dye then colors only the unwaxed areas, creating a pattern.

Bauhaus A famous art college in Germany that encouraged modern, industrial-style designs.

black hole A part of space where gravity is so strong that no light can escape.

blues American popular songs, often with sad words about love or poverty.

Bolshevik One of the group of Communists who played a part in the Russian Revolution of 1917.

Buddhism A religion based on the teachings of Prince Siddhartha Gautama, who lived in India around 550 B.C.

capitalism An economic system that encourages private ownership of land, homes, and businesses.

ceramic Made from baked clay.

Charleston An energetic American dance with fast, complicated footwork.

Christian A person who believes in the teachings of Jesus Christ, who lived in the Middle East around A.D. 30.

civilian A person who is not a member of the armed forces.

civil rights The rights of citizens, usually including the right to vote, receive an education, have a job, marry, and follow one's religion.

civil servants Officials in government departments.

civil war A war between rival groups within one country.

cold war The period of tension between the non-Communist Western nations and the Communist nations that lasted from 1947 to 1991.

collective farm A vast farm that is owned by the government.

colony A country ruled by a stronger foreign nation.

communism A system of government in which the state runs everything and nobody owns private property.

czar The title used by the emperors of Russia.

dictator A political leader who takes complete control of a country and rules alone.

empire A large area of land, including several different nations or peoples, governed by a single ruler called an emperor.

gravity The invisible force that pulls objects toward the center of the earth.

guerrilla A soldier who uses surprise tactics to fight against a stronger, better organized army.

Hindu A person who follows the Hindu religion, which grew up in India between 1500 and 600 B.C.

Holocaust The mass murder of Jews, Gypsies, and others by Adolf Hitler's Nazi party.

Homo erectus An extinct species of early people who lived from about 1.5 million to 300,000 years ago.

immigrant A person who moves to another country to live.

Impressionism A style of painting that creates images by using patterns of color, light, and shade.

irrigation Bringing water to dry land along specially built channels so that crops can grow there.

Islam The religion founded by Muhammad, a prophet who lived in Arabia from A.D. 570-632. It teaches that there is only one God, called Allah. Followers of Islam are called Muslims.

Jain A person who follows the teachings of a group of ancient

Indian religious teachers. Jains try not to harm any living creatures and to live pure, simple lives.

Jews Descendants of the Hebrew people who lived in parts of present-day Israel, Palestine, Syria, and Jordan around 1000 B.C., and who later settled in many parts of the world. Jewish people follow the religion of Judaism and observe many traditional customs.

kamikaze A Japanese pilot who dive-bombed allied warships during World War II, knowing that he would die on his mission.
kibbutz A communal farm run by Jewish settlers in Israel.

locomotive An engine that pulls railroad trains.

mandate An order or command.
matter The material from which everything in the universe is made. Matter itself is made up of tiny particles called atoms.
merino A breed of sheep that produces fine, silky wool.
missionary A person who tries to convert others to his or her own religious beliefs.
Morse code A code made up of long and short sounds (or flashes of light) that spell out letters and words. It is used to send messages.

nationalism Pride in and loyalty to one's country.
Nazism The beliefs of Nazis (members of the National Socialist German Workers' Party), who ruled Germany from 1933 to 1945. Nazis wanted to make Germany great, conquer more territory, and remove all non-Germans from their land.
Nobel Prize An important award given to people for outstanding contributions to science, medicine, literature, or world peace.

pacifist A person who believes that war is morally wrong.
paper A published lecture or essay.
Parsee A person in India who follows the religious teachings of Zoroaster, who lived in Persia about the seventh century B.C.
pasteurization Heating food to destroy germs.
plantation A big farm, often having just one kind of crop.
Prohibition Period in the U.S. (1920-1933) during which the sale of alcoholic drinks was banned.
propaganda Information that promotes a one-sided view.
property dealer A person who buys and sells houses and land.
Protestants Christians who belong to churches that broke away from the Roman Catholic Church in the sixteenth century.

Qing The dynasty that ruled China from 1644 to 1912.
quasar A very remote, bright object far away in space that sends out radiation as well as light.

rabies A deadly disease passed on by bites from infected animals.
racism Unfair treatment of people because of their race.
radioactive Emitting invisible rays.
Raj The lifestyle and political ideas of the British people who ruled India from 1857 to 1947.
rayon The world's first synthetic fiber, made from cellulose and acid. It was invented in 1884.
republican A person who supports a system of government in which leaders are elected by ordinary people, and there are no kings, queens, or emperors.
Roman Catholic A Christian who belongs to the church led by the Pope in Rome.

samurai An ancient Japanese warrior who followed a strict code of honor and bravery.
sharia Muslim law, which is based on the teachings of the Qur'an, the Muslim holy book.
Sikh A follower of the Indian religion founded by Nanak in the sixteenth century and which teaches belief in one God.
soviet The Russian word for "council." After 1917 it was used by Communists to describe the group that governed the USSR.
spiritual A religious song, often based on words from the Bible.
subcontinent A large land mass smaller than a continent; the Indian subcontinent contains modern India, Pakistan, Nepal, and Bangladesh.
Surrealism A style of art that creates distorted, dream-like images of people and objects.
synthetic Made in laboratories or factories rather than in nature.

transistor A miniature device used to carry electric current.

welfare state A country that provides benefits for citizens who are older, unemployed, or ill.
woodcut A picture created by carving a design in wood, covering the design in ink, then pressing paper on top.

X-rays Rays that can pass through flesh and clothes. They are often used to produce images of bones and other parts of the body.

Zionist A person who campaigned for a new nation to be created where Jewish people could live.

INDEX